My Blue Days Sound Like Blue Jays

Written by Amos Don

D1715275

In Loving Memory Of

*Mimose Don (R.I.P.) who always made sure
to remind me to think outside the box,
thus here I am...*

Acknowledgments

My gratitude most importantly goes to God. Faith has become the never-ending light burning on my heart's wick. I am very grateful for compassion and love over the years being the fruits of the Spirit moving supporters like Sophia; who has walked through the fire with me and became the blessing where I received my many literatures advancing my education to heights of transformation. Becoming friends with a published poet, Artem Vaskanyan; who inspired me with the reality of publishing his poem book "Ruminating Years" while incarcerated.

A special thank you, to my mother (Mimose) and grandmother (Simone) may they continue to rest in peace. Their words of wisdom continue to live in my heart. My mother always believed in me. Because of her constant encouragement to become a preacher, I write poetry to preach my inspired message. She didn't think twice about my method, encouraging me by letting me know that it was the same assignment. I have faith that if she was alive to see my accomplishment, today would be one of her joyful days on earth thanking God.

My son Christian, who gives me purpose to focus, my sisters (Nahomie, Dyna, and Rachelle), brother-in-laws (Patrick and Necasty), and all my nephews and nieces keep me alive as part of the family. My brothers (Volnaire and Esdras) keep me in mind, along with all my friends. Thank you all, and Joanna for seeing me worthy of a relationship.

Finally, but not least, my father (Voltaire), your love and forgiveness bring me peace.

Foreword

My wrongful conviction has made my life experience a lesson I've come to value. Before I saw life through eyes colored with ignorance, now I am able to see clearly and cherish it with all my heart. 'My Blue Days Sound Like Blue Jays' is about culture, love, despair, self-consciousness, sarcasm, political and spiritual intellectual growth. It consists of epic and short poems through which I reveal my life's struggles while living in Boston as a son to Haitian immigrants, and the real trauma Black Americans in the United States go through from past and current policies giving way to mass incarceration to policies where I've endured great suffering and loss. In the process, I was able to transform my failures, mistakes, and misfortunes into an achievement.

Please keep in mind I love the human race, and I am proud to be a born Haitian-American citizen. In fact, I'm empowered to be able to create a moment where I can get readers to reflect on themselves, my plight and also enjoy deep feelings even if they stir emotions of disgust and anger. I hope in those moments the readers can ask themselves "Why do I feel this way". Then I've fulfilled my purpose as a poet.

Sincerely,
Love & Respect
Amos Don

Blue Door

The heavens—
parted the sky,
Descending from a love—
Celestial ancestors only speak—
About a purpose I should fulfill—
With faith I can only see at this river—
Where God allowed a landing horse
with three pair of wings—
the color of dove,
A silent aura that sang—
A loud melody,
Stroking the strings of my heart—
Pure in comfort spirit,
Where I would be led
behind blue door waterfall,
and find new life
in the moral of a Ginen.

Public Bench, Love Only!

I rode a bench on the wind,
Feet planted on tiny sprinkled rocks— napping on dirt,
Where two doves— In human form
sat and allowed wind—
To kiss their lips as they spoke,
Of the sun and moon,
Both appearing in skies open room
before sun sets the mood—
Oblivious, of me observing;
Like a silent pigeon on a roof,
And upon the caesura between the two...
Arrived three pigeons in view—
Compelling one of the wrist of the two—
Flicking dancing treats from compassion,
While me—
As the only Black canary on this bench,
Reflects on a moment
we have overcome.

The Black Sea

Release: such burden of fear,
in the hands of ocean kissing feet,
And at the edge—
Where clouds caress the sky to smile above,
Then,
Will wings of peace descend
upon the mind,
and hearts will stroke into tears—
On sea of faces—
Upon how the spirit of love
laps towards, Ussssssssss.

Dancing Candle

In the flesh: this night burned auspiciously
under a single candle—
Where three footsteps of dropped water
meets coffees,
Coe... Coe... Coe—
The Knocks from Angels,
Enters where human hades
was suppose to be,
But in trance my body spins
on open arm's love,
Where confinements
four cornered cell became lights
full moon sphere;
Be that as it may—
For the naked eye—
See I,
speaking to I—
Really is not what it appears to be.

Norfolk Season's

October in this place—
Again settles itself
in a robe of discomfort,
and more of the same spirits in here
dangles on the edge of sleeves—
In relation to
what concerns the hearts avalanche;
Like those who believe in the foundation
of trees that produce beautiful harvest leaves,
Swaying beautifully,
Until wind blows, and shows—
Where we Fall
there's no branch to hang by the neck on,
Mist in the air—
Drizzle down in kissing raindrops,
Fogging the buzzing sounds of lawn mowing—
Mixing with the voices
tuning another's singing lyre,
About summers sentiment memories' souvenirs—
Birds and the bees,
A distance becoming clear it's freezing,
Thanksgiving without the children—
Brings wonders about Jesus in Christmas—
And here goes winter
colder in New Years—
Amongst hearts wishing better results
in our judicial system—
Designed for economic reasons,
rather than—
Compassion spring gives the victors victims—
When April's eyes shower
and bring May flowers—
Reversing cases of sadness
to summer happiness—

Mosquitoes sting to live with;
Like freedom we seek every Norfolk Season's.

Sweet Violin Sound

As the pallbearers carry off my days,
I lay on the sound of spanking wind—
Stroking the melodies
of my conscious self into tears,
For I can see what purpose means,
While inferno realm knows satisfaction—
I can only see what could have been;

Like a feather slowly descending
from the fallen wing I imagine
slowly stroking under my chin;
like a gentle brushing of a silent violin...

Hills Of Calvary

On the mound,
I see Glory—
Tap dancing in joy
across faces who reach—
A light,
On the other side of life—
Yet,
I endure sorrow's bitter sweat—
With lame ankles battling up hill,
Where journey cease—
For idling pain,
But faith shouts—
"CRAWL ON BENDING KNEES!"
And like the Holy Spirit in Him—
I arrive.

One Step At A Time

Eyes open after a taste
of Eve's apple left over—
In modern days
dead faces on green paper—
Led me in places
Devil destroys Gods favorites.
Too weak to gain courage—
Birth father thinks Larry is my destruction—
No knowledge I was his road
to State and Fed charges,
See why I admire him—
Avoiding my self-destruction.
Pretty womens was what I lusted,
With a booty was just a bonus—
And no brain gave them sexual exposure,
Knowing mama would never condone her,
But money gave you her number—
Now on route to dead faces
the way the world earn faces—
Definition why they're on currencies.
Locked away—
For how comfortably I got paid,
Now pays for the knowledge
on how to escape when I pray—
Clearly seeing who stayed,
With loyalty— I'll pay,
Sticking with them
one step at a time.

Black African Diamond

Rare diamond is the likes of you—
BLACK
but shines; like you—
African jewel,
Haitian roots—
Rough edges making you enticing but
PRICELESS!
Foreign land she shines—
As if still in her mother's land,
Won't betray herself
and lower her worth—
Shine she Shine;
Like the Black Diamond from Africa—
In face and hand of strangers
playing with her heart.

FLOWER

Beauty in you lay in your womb—
In light, what makes you a women,
Same power God gives a rose
to blossom through fertilizing—
Understand why men give women flowers?
But just like a flower—
A seed is needed to start life,
Blossom that comes from water
the planter pours into the root;
like a soul need love
to pour when a seed is planted.
There is no secret
or mistake
how a flower grows—
Make no mistake how children will grow.

Misery Loves My Company

Misery appearing like the reaper,
Away with my love—
I'm left disgust,
Pain now lingers
when my eyes shut—
Flashing moments,
Arms pinned open wide
sacrifice for loves sexual fire—
But misery, is the cause
I'm reflecting what was,
Reason the friends I often called—
Envious of your blush,
and wanted you crush—
Whispering such things
lynching my heart
for my company it loves.

Gift To Have A Girl

How many single water drops
in a single cell
have to sound like I'm lonely here,
Sweets are decaying my health
wallowing from hurt
I'm not comforting a girl,
Lending her my ears
understanding what vice versa means;
too many medication given for depression—
When I'm willing to hear
Longing
for a man's touch deriving from love—
Nectar
Raw chocolate leaves on the tongue,
because down below has it all—
And I'm addicted
to when the rain falls
just as you are,
Imagination is taking me too far—
Repeating many moons without the stars
wishing I could play a part—
That picks flowers
for every broken heart,
Where I train men in a fortress
reflecting Wonder Woman's world
preparing to engage love
to a specific girl across the world—
Destroying the villan of lust,
Trust—
I'm equipped to love,
From long labor cells produced
in my mental health—
Link to increasing
a women's pituitary gland

conversing with them—
Understanding a relax woman
makes the button easier to press,
Far from a large boat that sails—
But Pisces birth flows naturally
swimming with the motion the ocean gives—
Awareness to body's sensitive to answers
that lead to treasures from crevices,
Lesson women always mentions
I care to listen—
Like Superman saves the world
because of two women—
And I stand with the ladies
attacked in Gamer Gates—
BECAUSE
Behind bars you'll learn
men play all the games,
and threats are only real
when you attempt,
But like Hulk—
Every women gives me a calm
Scarlett Johansson could,
Street value weakens
to stand for female virtue—
Intensifying dishonesty
crippling many with manipulation
from jealousy—
Thoughts of woman
may not have wanted me enough—
Insecurity, egotistical, self-destructing me,
But with strength found—
The cupid moves are uplifting women,
Charismatically
without falling under hashtags—
Pointing at Weinstein,
I was baptized in compassion

that always sounded poetic,
And Phenomenal Women—
Is the cause
I'm eager to escape these bars
romance by a pond like swans—
Until every women experience
Jada Pickett's feeling
in Jason Lyrics—
Can't help but to fall,
because I'm vulnerable to love,
and specific has no voice—
Big, Tall, Or small,
Deserves what oxytocin cause
when kissing is done—
Transforming frogs into love doves
bringing olive branch
to female's world—
Plucked from this heart of mines,
Similar to gardens of Eden—
Canceling out preference superficial has—
On which girl I would rather make smile,
See I'm a cub that's lost
until Nala show's my place as a lion—
The drip drops,
Will it eventually stop,
As I scramble my thoughts
still locked in a box—
Waiting for a women's response
to end my lonely thoughts...

Urban Revolver

Windowpane from my angelic eyes—
As an adolescent,
Mesmerized on how the open sky
would pepper down snow without a blink
from my eyes—
Those crystal flakes would land
and convert into liquid dirt,
Flowing down where many reside
in pothole infested communities—
Labeled as urbans.
With each kiss of sun
passing through the next days
dressing the neighborhood
in overdose empty crack viles
as if a silent plague—
Tiptoed onto the backs of the inner cities,
Where as a child—
Oblivious to paraphernalia evidence
is where we innocent urban angels congregated
and played kickball or stickball,
A living rabbit amongst a pack of fox—
Before naive cornered my back;
like a feline kitten—
At the bosom of broken glass ally,
Where my prehistory urban dinosaur
appeared himself—
Cultivating the green grass
of my youthful mind
into overbearing steam stench sewers—
Dripping drops of poison
every second after another—
Till this manipulation gave birth
to every unconscious decision
rotating my six cylinder revolver

conceived with one loaded seed—
The product I've become,
Compliments of my environment—
Click!
The cylinder shifts clockwise
towards the counter clock time—
I became victim to the glamorous
lure of video games—
Allowing an older teen
to reap what he sowed,
Whisking away my sexual innocence
the early age of ten—
Mental and physical molestation;
This past image replaying
in a flaming dance in my head—
So his neck rested in violent comfort
in between the pillow of my hands—
Clamp tightly together,
YET!... He lives
by the mercy of Angel's symphony—
Reaching from out the tonsil cave
of my mother's scream, to BREATHE!...
So I released,
And ocean tears
from the rivers of my trauma,
Click!... High school dropout
Click!... Violent crimes
Click!... Drug distribution—
The same cylinder cycle spins,
But rather than a pedophilia—
I inherited the volcanic atmosphere
of a Petro believer—
Who now roamed on concrete jungle communities
with a group of prides—
All lacking the clouds wisdom
to rise as a King

and envision the warm dwelling
of a single mother as a sanctuary—
Planting sunflower seeds
on the fertile grounds
of her three son's mind—
Instead of the product
of my dark alley life handed down
from one urban dinosaur to a next,
As the last Click!...
Takes the life of a child in a man—
Demonstrating reverse contrast
effect before cause—
The final trigger
pulled by a Prosecutor's hand.

Mothers Summer Temperature

Invading fingertips—
Appearing to be the first aliens
that is to say
whisked me out of planet womb
and into a universe umbilical cord
is no longer the key—
Steering mother's ship to sweat,
Resembled as mist perspiring down—
Clouds of hair matted on mother's
African mountainous forehead
while giving birth,
But that was spring of eighty-six,
And this was summer of ninety-six—
Kissing my chubby cheeks
with plenty premature pubic free mentality—
Sniffing around like a puppy
dumb enough to chase a tail
connected to—
Coming off a porch
before the daylight of thirteen—
Mothers inauguration to nightmare
on Elm Street's way of thinking,
Realizing kidnappers can be real,
The innocence
of my chunky penguin walking baby,
Drowning me in river of worries—
Bladder—
Knocking my knees
in the rhythm of having to piss,
Mahogany thighs squeezing
because the toilet seat isn't right,
and not enough window time
to keep an eye on the inconsiderate child—
Chubby handsome baby

stumbling her African feet—
As if back in Haiti
dancing the beat
off nervous heartbeat
while she sit and piss—
Wondering if she'll see
her seed smoking a stick—
Certain she seen,
Pants sagging
modern African male tribe—
Wrapping his arm around her child,
Conning him from wisdom
Voltaire gave to him as a child—
Smoking!
Hoping not,
All through a window scene—
My blood pressure
doesn't become summer's temperature.

Loves Common Side Effect

As the love season sickness begins,
Hugs can only comfort
the shivering it brings—
Damn!
Another snot bubble face,
and my reaching
is a second from a tumble—
Off the edge
where I lay on a bed dressed in pajamas
starting to smell like sweat,
And my guess—
Seems to believe it's the box of kleenex
being carried backward by ants—
As I watch
my fingers playing piano in the air,
But then this headache
doesn't help things appearing straight—
Because the constant door knocking
and asking; "ARE YOU THERE!"
Ignored for the thinking—
It's the avalanche
that rocks the pounding in my head—
Apparently
from the fall that was evident off the bed—
I think I see birds,
But instead
it's twinkle stars flashing
with the cameras gone,
Love's hunger is the cause
my buttocks numb—
From failed attempts to walk
on wobble legs that dance;
like baby horses first steps,
At worst—

My health seems to reflect
this apple on my chair
becoming a science fair— Project,
Perhaps a bite,
The symbol of a light bulb
pauses my life—
Then scratch through tangled hair,
Chuckling out realization
the flu... uhmm, can't be right—
Because of the mind
flirting with memory
of that last bite—
Is where I sat flashing back
why my heart
panicked on attack—
She was no longer mine.

Even Though L.T.'M.E. (Love Through My Eyes)

This point of convergence
staring into the pupil of my soul,
Hollows inside of a distance
hand in hand board walking—
Toes fanning off sand; even though

I'm in prison,
I positioned your heart
to build an igloo
under chilling gravesite drifts—
Causing your breath of happiness
to become faint
around the realm of domestic hurricane— Ambushing
your trust each fall
for another after me,
Destiny seeking to fend
for the grass endowed with beauty
of our children,
Because I
in favor of street's intimacy—
Nightmare dreams,
Now resort on a hill opposite of Malibu,
and you as my coconspirator—
Strike down with a life sentence
nurturing my half of humans responsibility—
Enduring the rise of one
having to be defiant
as a single mother; even though

I'm cursed
deceased in physique—
Rather
reborn in spirituality behind barriers—
Instead
My overflowing eyes

are buried in oceanic haze of fog—
Seems to be
my weeping reason as a ghost,
I hover around
wishing I listened—
How your heart mentioned
"gang banging, leaves you and the children victims"
To whispers caressing where I'm missing—
With another baby... baby... baby
your friends gangbang to mourn you—
Copulating me romantically; even though

I'm an inebriated bottle nose—
That I know,
Deems me unworthy
than the withering bones of dead beats—
When liquor's dizzy spell
reveals the true man I should be,
and the courage to speak—
The coward in me
leaving you secluded in the flesh—
With the constant morning melody of infants
to silence in bosoms nutrition,
Clothe in care's heart beat
on many, many yesterday's dirty sleeve—
Stenched in bad odor of shame—
Knowing your the Wom-and-Man
in my reality; even though

Treading water in somber reflection—
The eve of my redemption
understood single motherhood,
Many, Many generations

under the star clouded moon—
Planet earth is really you,
Rotating alone under sun's seducing heat—

Producing season's to birth
grasses
creeks singing around trees—
Creating apple for the breast feeding
of all living being—
A single mother of nature.

Letter To A Poetic Realm
(R.I.P. 7-25-19)

Beyond where you now linger
as an ancestor—
I remain on doors opposite side knocking,
Your days no longer whisper by in pain,
Yet the ones here with I—
Grief at my smile,
Hearing the harmony of waterfalls—
Splashing
with the sounds of amazing grace—
Where I am in captivity; like a slave,
I've come to find a love
for family on both
mother and father's side
swimming in the oceans of Haiti.
Looking back upon
plagues me—
Sickness in thoughts
of my overdue correspondence,
My yearn hope you'll accept
with hugs open arm,
Ritual belief—
Words I speak
dancing the symphony echoes
water courses through your mind—
Where roots become quench
from heart's fertile grounds,
Rainbow shooting ends
meeting centered love—
Dearly missed,
Moments moving in sloth replay;
Like a butterfly
dancing with wind...
"Action Of Grace"

God knowing if I could—
Running to perform the steps of conga—
For your embrace;
like warm blanket comforts—
Image preferred to never forget,
Rather this aching sob ruminating—
A chance chirping words
with aunt ancestors I could of have,
Perhaps if free from the chains
of American vanity—
In order to see—
Without the sprinting streams
of family love—
Wither away the roots;
Like a soundless leaf
descends off a branch—
Then whisk away violently,
In hope
my kissing gesture
carry into your days,
and whet morning to blush sunlight—
Where you now live.

When Birds Sing

I heard a bird sang this morning,
The same sound I feel eternally.
My vision was blurry,
but where I live there's no hurry—
So I envisioned Mimose speaking to me
like butterflies flap their wings easily—
Mentioning
beauty seeks you to ease angers misery.
A circle represents infinity,
Your destiny to be in society—
Revealing how to end
scrutinizing Black and Browns
in order to see
what communities are producing.
I'm philosophizing
what skeptics ignore to be true.
My wisdom wings
have given me virtue
to share with you.
Value peace,
Love to value—
No longer repeating the same jail bird songs,
Free your spirit
from what they sentenced you to physically.
When anger is consuming—
Awareness is at its peak
to avoid acting stupidly—
Transcending you into a visionary
releasing anger poetically—
Which makes you the worst enemy politically,
because bombs like you
affects the lives
White Supremacy's design to not see—
Restoring Justice,

Now a part of you—
Proves reflection
like Christ mid-thirties,
Gaining patience—
Philosophizing the world is family,
Faith conceiving one to see spiritually—
Heed the conversation on the ship
which freed the slaves back centuries,
Embrace the actions universe speaks
through sign language—
You shall witness,
In you the gifts God instilled—
Explaining the song a bird sang
about community healing–
With Restorative Justice being the key.

What Is Your Name?!

Without the mane—
I journey onto Lyon, Street
under moving stars
blushing with cupid's grin—
At a forest
consist of traffic lights
and scrambling sewer rats torpedoing
in and out of weekly warm trash,
For an encounter
with lust serenading desire
the heart feels—
Awaiting
A nubian Queen—
Bedazzling my intricate hairs
to rise skin's goosebump mounds—
Causing my roars;
like a jungle King—
Echoing off the night walls
now on Bailey, Street—
The way her bare sugar brown skin
lie down on cool air—
Consuming the silk sheets;
Like a black panther
on an Amazon tree,
With emerald gem eyes—
She visualizes confidence in me,
But I couldn't believe in pyramids
this beautiful in my own dreams—
Sculpted in soft smooth thighs,
Traveling derriere's mountain peak
full of moon—
Shining areolas horizon erection
over deserts breast,
As dawn accepts my paws—

Palming where the heart beats...
What is your name?!
While head lowered under showers nose—
Staring at the drain,
WHAT... IS... HER... NAME.?!

The Avenue Of Home Street Rada

Homes Ave: Nestles somewhere
in Dorchester quietly
Yet!
Surely as seduction can be
stroke of six caress the clock,
The breaking of dawn—
Sets the ripen puberty
of young black souls
into frenzy motion—
In pursuit of finery
amongst other lost tribes shopping—
For a night the caesura in between
Boom... Boom... Boom...
Are urban princesses—
Twisting hips in diety waves
without the essence of yoga—
But rather from the breast of folklore,
Where black warriors and Kings
Possess a gripping on vibrating waist,
Bantu's pure spiritual protector ship—
Whereas the knee normally buckles up,
Boom... Boom... Boom...
Appears the spirit of Bantu Rada—
Slowing party atmosphere in trance;
like ceremony... Erzulie!

Morning Nightmares

The sound in connection with keys
frustrates from startled sleep—
Now that the brush of my teeth
has become dreary traditions for war—
Rather than a special speech,
What hell it is
walking disgracefully towards a table
used for purpose accomplishing
J. Edgar Hoover's segregation—
My own race before the sweet joy
of an apples morning taste,
Numerically enslaving me
with OH-three-eight (038)—
Affirming oxymoron continuance
on our mental state—
Observing individuals discriminate,
but agree with "CNN" case,
Racism exists if one have black face,
Whichever is causing acts on a land
derogatorily named
"Negro Mountain"
Hazelton, West Virginia that mirrors
jurors on Michael Brown's case—
With repeating mornings
sounding like Eric Garners
"I CAN'T BREATHE"
Thus from within confinement
I hold mines—
So another brother won't lose theirs.

How Much A Visit Cost

This cost gripping my soul inspite
identically the strength a mother
holds her still born,
But far up a river
where tiresome awaits—
Stamina's only source to love,
Connecting me physically
with my birth mother at one-O'clock—
Concentrated in a camp
from the likes of Germans and Americans—
Once prejudice against Jewish and Asians,
Now Blacks and Hispanics,
The self knowledge slaying me to see
noose I tossed over a tree with blunder—
Compelling my days to face
walls I can reach
across from where I sit—
For the purpose
displaying my Black Bird heart denuded—
Rather atoning feathers I plucked,
Instead—
The applause exist solely
short on a clock
constantly falling behind—
A decision torturing me universally,
Addiction needing mother's affection on time—
Liberating me.

My Roots Planted

Haitian raised
eating mango and sugar cane—
Is no wonder why my hips
squeeze the sweet juice of tango
with the Dominicano's,
The essence of Petro
makes me multicultural in every sense—
Originating from Congo,
Loving beats that start
with Boom-Boom-Bo—
My women's with high cheek bones,
Soft side for poor folks—
Especially
Starving children in third world countries,
Tired
Conservatives living racist mentally—
Afro Americans not knowing
their own strength,
Religions not at peace—
Am I designing clouds of illusionary Zzzz's
boring one to sleep;
Like hibernating bears?
Perhaps excuse of half our country—
So I look to you,
No! Nooo!
Not you—
But the one who spoke
to a cherries heart from seed
now it blossoms with sweetness
every harvest season;
like I witness in Haitians
when we listen,
and unity blooms fruit—
Where my Kreyol

ballet's on my accent—
Expressing how the seed
rooted within me was planted well.

Coming Of Age

They thought that my life was over
but everything that I've endured
has made me a soldier.
Far from broken
which was the goal
of those who lusted after my soul.
These walls and steel have grown familiar.
I am a man,
a human and not a killer.
This is the reason for my smile,
A smile which originated
from the spirit that they sought to break,
A smile that they wanted to take
which is the intention of this place
contrary to popular belief.
They can not give me
what the most high gave
"LIFE"
nor can they reduce me
to a modern day slave.
I am dead
when I have No voice,
No choice and No remorse
therefore I am alive
vocal and hopeful.
WHAT?
You thought I would wither and crumble
like a leaf
under the pressure of political heat?
Especially in the face of beasts
who have a history of feasting
on the flesh of the weak and poor,
Like an eagle, I soar
and like a lion I roar

from the cage of righteous rage.
This has been my rite of passage
yes, my coming of age...

First Amendment

Gruffness is the attitude always perceived—
When souls diagnose
with Affirmative-Bloodline speaks,
Were it not that—
Naked trauma burdens me,
Supposing one should understand
why egg yolks cracked onto my skin
can quickly sizzle into scramble,
Savoring the taste of words
compelling brains to rattle,
Rushing scientist
to the assistance of oppressors—
For the surety under microscope
This "DNA"
Impregnating the world's atmosphere
has no relation to Martin Luther king—
Unveiling how America's
four fathers imprisoned us,
Utilizing Justice with the same intentions
gangbangers attack rivalries—
All the same,
With loaded hollow Prosecutor's
and AK-47 Judges—
Hair pin happy,
Behold on a Pale Horse
condemning me a somatic death,
And more of the same persons
hearing me vent—
Is family needing me free,
Unintentional premeditated loaded seeds—
Growing generation of bias towards
"Star Spangled Banner"
On which occasion knowing I—
Relate to taking accountability

actions leading back to slavery's 13th Amendment,
Yet can not ignore in court
same bible sworn to tell the truth—
Forgiveness is not considered too,
My humble self
not in the least, killed—
Like victim's families intentions
envision my dangling legs
lifeless from a tree—
On the other hand
the system of snitches-get-stiches
kept me in a valley
the shadows of death—
For I feared evil and didn't tell,
Intelligibly what the judicial system can tell—
Undeveloped brain was really the case
falling short of courage to say
"I'M AFRAID"
Its always been the same
since the fifth grade—
My neighborhood cultivate minds
the wrong way,
Pretender reaping root crops
fitting with bullies,
Avoiding them picking me as the plague—
Infecting soft hearts to become harden,
But alternatively—
They indicted me like the courts did,
Peer pressure causing me to endure
affects marijuana entertain
when police sirens ring—
PTSD—
Tricking myself to believe
friends fire gunshots near the ears—
Innating one with symptoms
Bipolar and Schizophrenia—

Still today I'm ashamed of,
Not more than keeping silence
for bullets that I imagined
smooching me to my death—
Giving forth a speaking sound,
Valor beyond the call of duty,
Scent of newborn babies breath—
The freedom of speech gives,
This petition for Government to redress
what peer pressure unjustly made them neglect
when it came to my case.

Black Crow

Black crow—
Can this be
your loud cry
derives from outcomes of ebony feathers—
Familiar
My everyday seems to harmonize
such a sound in the likes—
To Maya Angelou's
"Why the Caged bird sings"
Questioning freedom—
My wonders,
Life around doves—
Is such
beautiful open sky under the sun—
Segregated,
The plight of Ravens weeping
tones of Nina Simone—
"Mississippi Goddam!"
As my reflection to Massachusetts—
"Goddam!"
On this concrete sky that I tread,
Painted close to blue skies—
Due to white clouds
constant rain on Black Lives,
Whitewashing our wail of woes
stained in blood
Yet!
I still wonder how your wings would look
surrounded by America's bald Eagles—
In ways the gloss of our arms
rise in submission
preserving the black crystal feathering our skin,
Are the Red Robin's gone
like most of our Native tribes down here?

OH Black Crow,
Why does your wailing–
Alone on this tree
reminds me of strange fruits... All over again?

My Burden Train

Distance upon Distance
as the acacia trees
run pass my fogging window—
Where I sit forehead against fiberglass
on a neverending ride,
Until—
Awed in my stillness,
Breath held
keeping my window cleared—
Long enough to observe
this train in opposite direction,
Halting minds boarded to stop,
As the doors opened up—
Air between our realms entered,
Whispering passion touching my lips—
My ancestor now boarded on my train—
Causing random stops
to become exit destinations,
False beliefs that boarded my mind—
Sacred for butterflies and green grass
where Nile rivers run wild—
Goodbye, Goodbye
This old man rise
with one foot the size of an elephant's thighs
approaching the next stop,
but to my surprise
a wife accompanied him—
Dragging a chained dog
shaking his head no,
Perhaps on my train
I was his slave—
Goodbye, Goodbye
As a young man rise,
and slang talks—

"I Love You Dog"
But in that thought—
The voice of a female scatters it,
Questioning my manhood
while she tags along with two girls—
Nose rings
pierced on like Bull(ies),
But freedom had nothing to prove—
I peppered over her seasoning salt
with universal love,
And she new her ride was also up—
Goodbye! Goodbye!
My ancestor—
Came to halt my burden train.

All Roads

Can this be?
I sailed before the wind—
Allowing your journey
on the sea of love
to lie an anchor—
Over boarding down your cheeks,
Weathering—
Storm overcasting your best view
against my better breeze of judgment—
Keeping your heart unsteady
from selfish detour,
Where clouds become grey,
and constant lightning
hammers across open sky—
Once full of sun rays,
Resembling a familiar smile,
CAN THIS BE!
Moment differed—
Outpouring our emotions
over dirt road's Dead End—
Existence to roots,
Traveling avenues oblivious,
Hearts fighting to keep true—
Shackled in distance isolated pain,
This road drowning love boats
at the entrance our rivers paved.

Joe And Nah

Like a ladybug—
She descends,
and upon my hand
she finally rest,
Consoled in the water my eyes float—
Awakening her polka-dotted wings.

Cotton Mouth

Twilight in my head
Heavy on a tongue in thirst
Yen for expression.

Ginen

Tranquility is a language—
Grandmother spoke outloud,
How cloud's musical pause—
Were thunders way of applauding
understanding I now saw—
Rain in baptizing matrimony
with Blue Jay's trumpet beak,
Caress with the lips—
The ears romancing with intertwine hands,
Who parted sea,
and allows dreams to speak—
Of earth under bare feet
being foundation tomorrow need
to plant a better me.

What Love Offers

Celebrating arm to arm
link with children singing—
We Are The Future,
Allows happiness to offer
pain a glass of water
choosing to listen—
Pick flowers
before seeing picking cotton,
Taste the river of your wine
before finger pointing
at cups others drink by—
Dream, dream
the mark of affection
bringing nightmare thoughts
into green grass picnics under the sun—
Rest your heart on conga drums,
and enjoy the symphony beat
hands perform,
Being you, or me—
Reaching where colors has no image,
because marriage proposals
to equalities reasons—
Savor the salty tears,
Then add the world's amount of sugar—
Smiles,
Becoming the ears of a babies soul
so Angel's can talk—
Change today, tomorrow... OR Now!

Beautiful Fetus

Looking back in wonder
the eyes you may of have,
Can't ignore—
Birds it could of drawn,
Words making me cry—
Lacking the wisdom
of burning flambeau's third eye,
Knowledge sickening me with chills;
like anemia brings—
Support I should've given,
I'm bleeding from this—
When babies cry,
and I see wings—
Tormenting me with honesty,
What could of been—
Searching through the landscape of my mind,
God reveals how they forgave
abortion I asked—
Junior or Amillia
He or She—
Could of been cure
helping human nature breathe
healing we need—
Grief,
Also reason my knees
are numb from praying—
For children and every women's
No matter the religion,
Let Angel's sing
my ballard lamentation
of my beautiful fetus—
Realizing suggesting
their abortion was my sin,
Hoping you now find peace—

Forgiving my life with tears
God filled the oceans with.

The End Of Love Burns: Cigarette & Sex

A few width off from being—
In sync in between two fingertips visually,
Engages my mind
in ménage-a-trois mentally—
Essentially
because lips that blow
wind from deep inhales—
Know sensitive spots;
Like skin on inner thighs
bear witness—
When licking causes affects
that cough up Ooooo's and Ahhh's
the smoke in lung gives—
For holding breath anticipating
in the other hand—
A sip of red wine,
Cool chills
reapplying wet lips
to wrap around such stick—
Burning with the same warmth
fired up between my other lips—
When I flick
bringing bliss
following the trace of smoke—
Designing halos above my dream,
Staring back down
on top of me—
Only a butt of cigarette,
Remembering
how sex with love feels.

Youth In Mission

Clapping laughter present itself
on the faces of Haitians—
Reflecting Bantu's circle
African girls
with barrett's on their hair—
Forgetting that the van they ride in,
A sixteen passenger—
Now fueled with a choir
Consist of
Soprano, Alto and Tenor,
Speaking acappella language
that birds can answer to—
As doves design a crown of light
following flocks singing gospel songs,
Coloring the avenue hills blue
when the tenors chime along;
like a pack of wolves
howling under full moon—
Bliss that continue to taste;
like banana split
on tongues
speaking about Jesus
on a sundae—
Causing interior windows to fog,
and oblivious to all—
Stumbling around drunk praising drugs
on street corners left and rights turn on—
Where porch lights are the eyes congregated,
Wondering are we high?
As this van passes by;
like meteor across the sky,
If only they were wise and followed
the one star that rose in Bethlehem
known as Immanuel—

All the reason why
Youth In Mission
drove around to minister.

A Flowers Path

I'm not the aroma
that lingers in the summer air—
OR the pain that's tolerable
when someone's laying peacefully
on burial ground—
Instead I'm the feelings,
When I come whipping
from behind someone's back smiling—
Feeling he or she receives me,
Feeling—
I am fed water in the evenings,
and keep men and women into me—
I'm not a Lily
nor a Daffodil,
Not even Rose's split personality—
Just the path flowers come across.

I Know You!

I know you!
Your not clothe with Adonai,
and in fact—
I accept you with the passion
Christ carried the cross,
Abiding how you make me feel,
Only molds my intuition
with the understanding—
How an angel can fall
without spiritual wings—
Filling my head
with questions to seek,
But my heart giggles with tears—
How dare you make me feel heartsick,
Material things—
Yes
the picket fence make sense,
but not more than
"In God We Trust"
on currency rather than the currency itself—
See!
I know you—
You whispered about truth being weak—
Causing all Judas
to think love of money
worth more than what he believed—
And now your here
tormenting depression on me,
But my mirror reflects trinity—
How my wrist clockwise the volume
hearing Tasha Cobb scream—
BREAK EVERY CHAIN!
Suddenly the phone rings,
and divine intervention speaks

through my sibling—
Inspiration I give them
comes from my mental stability—
Quenching their soul spiritually,
What more do I need—
I know you,
Your not the peace
Bantu's Jesus brings me—
Exodus through an open sea,
Curing disease like leprosy,
Legacy for my seed—
I know you,
And by grace
I know you'll never win.

My 1-800 Start With 617

My Logic features, Fabiola—
In a constant state
where feathers are chanting
to keep me from accepting
journey Aaron Hernandez chose
hanging up dearly departed–
Pending investigation on
"Global Tel"
"Securus"
Profiteering—
Kicking chair from under me
every twenty minutes
hanging up on me—
Leaving sunny domain cloudless,
For I'm accepting
the way I'm falling—
Facing the sky,
because the concrete awaiting
is rather swords that will fear
the pain wanting to die,
and I wonder why—
Commissary allows the order of one
Diphenhydramine bottle—
Which has potential to keep me asleep
speaking to my son freely
drinking plenty pills
drowning me in a sea of dreams—
Kicking sand
holding Fabiola and Christian's hand,
After hearing a teacher my skin—
Bullying my kid,
Rather
Teaching bombs should never
come near human teeth,

And reason his sisters father not his—
Because love created him first,
But tone operator interrupts—
Diggs me a grave
buried alive near decaying bones
with tear stains visible enough—
Explaining how people feel
alone here in Dante's inferno world,
Only when I feel like dying
missing life past by
with Christian riding his first bike—
Ironically
what keeps me alive—
Long enough to dial his mother's number
just to hear them say "Hi!"
Forgetting I want to die,
Despite committing the only crime
Fabiola pushed our love aside—
A love Christian perhaps
search alone for at night,
Because to many voices repeating—
You look more like your dad,
Compliments—
Why this razor is digging into my wrist
where vertical line cuts over
vein connected to my heart,
And today's call—
Was enough to know
next call derives from motivation
Logic express—
About not wanting to die anymore
hearing my past life repeating
through Christian's mind—
Unloved feelings by peers
in fifth and fourth grade
reflecting the Hispanic

that stole my innocence—
Seeking friendship from peers
before establishing
what that means with siblings—
Ignoring,
Speaking back to parents
leads you to loneliness
quicker than isolation does in prison...
Yesterday,
I wanted to die Christian,
But my 1-800 start
with your— 617.

Love Like River Flow

As the river flows
I seek to stream love
like it shows—
Compassion no matter the animal,
Wildlife is welcome to drink
as much as the last—
Sat drinking by the riverflow;
like every human capturing fish to feast—
Then forgiving that human
for that fish I helped live—
I'm in search of this,
Where one may believe has no possibility,
but then again—
Bantu tribe say
Jesus did this in his sleep,
and that's the life I seek—
Where I dont feel
I would rather save my mother
before my brothers
or sisters before my father,
If life gave me a reason
to make a last minute decision,
Disappointment—
Slaying my heart slowly,
When only I want to love
every living thing equally,
but feelings keep me connected
deeper than I see,
and I feel—
I still love my mother
more than my brothers,
and my sisters—
The reason my heart
would brake after my decision—

Can this be a gift I question,
Or just the way
the devil defeats me,
because I care,
More for another rather equally,
The reason I can't see me—
Kissing the cheeks of my nieces
with the same compassion
I do with my son Christian—
OR the heart to speak about love
in the midst of two individuals I know
assaulting the one I know I love more,
This love I seek—
Even when I speak
should make one feel
from accidental spit on skin;
like this river satisfy thirst—
My soul,
Knows love
individuals differently.

To Speak My Last In Song

As Jagged the edges of my heart is—
With you,
I only knew this to be true,
The twinkle beat
sounding like stars
tap dancing our beginning—
Feels like I
"Walked outta Heaven"
Now that I'm not with you,
But as the beat continues
off teardrops tapping
on earth's drums under feet—
Only proves,
How lonely looks,
living beautifully
with love still running through me,
Causing wilderness space psychologically
becoming fruits producing long rivers
my soul fishes through—
Linking memories that had meaning
many moons ago
from a singing sparrow left humming
voice message tunes
that whispered Mariah's
"WE BELONG TOGETHER"
Stored subconsciously—
Adele in me,
HELLO—
From a side
acknowledging broke your heart—
Securing my trust
on how handsome I was,
Now agony tortures
how ugly that was—

When in fact astrology lined me
with galaxy's heart—
Accepting the flaw in my draws,
With cabinets full of more—
Including how I pigeon toe walked myself
into a realm,
Where pigeons land to be fed
by human pigeons,
Ways you once shared freely,
Your extended hand,
For a knee to land on my end,
But mercy preserved me a healing hand—
Pictured with a million open arm garments
the color snow falls—
In tune with clapping reminisce,
Awareness—
Even on last rose pedals
between your beauty
and I the beast—
Love symbolize purpose
To speak my last in song,
"WE BELONG TOGETHER".

(SMU) Special Managing Unit

Exorcism or incantation
of hocus-pocus I wonder?
As the bottom of my feature
hangs in awe
certain in what they need—
Like Roman Catholics
busy oneself with,
Whereupon I see
the spirit of a man feed off feces,
and function in it;
like God cursed the souls of pigs—
In face of brass
the total disregard for a river that run red,
Blood God cleansed our misdeeds with,
Whenever the ritual work of art
wasteland slitting their wrist—
Writing symbols on walls
with relation to identifying
by means the devils identity,
Active—
In filth without integrity,
Just simply if their mothers could see
the labor rage destroying sheets
that keep them warm on cell beds—
Pitching food
in ways of a wishing well they now accept
out of same toilet bowl we piss,
Who can they be—
When inhabitants of pandemonium
take over their mental capacity—
Yet sanctitude flickers
a candlelight behind pleading eyes,
Where I stopped in my chilling skin
knowing the remedy they needed

I lacked to unfreeze it—
So does the Doctors and Psychologists
offering romantic dates
with sedative hypnotic overdosing love—
When compassion has the passion
flirting with Elohim—
Additionally to stroke a brush of touch
alongside their cheeks—
Seeing their no different from me,
Peace only exist
if they have faith in him—
Engaging my ego
in wedlock intimacy
with Seraphim—
Angel of love,
Prepared
to redeem from—
Devils captivity.

Prison Desert

This single walk thirst me;
like a dry pavement
on deserts blind alley,
"WHO AM I"
The inner self express
to thoughts blowing by—
Begging the sun with open arms,
Touch my root;
like the branches on a tree grows,
"HOW FAR CAN THIS WATER WAY GO"
Burning up in exhausting wonder
as I think of my inner nature
down wash in stream
off the sides of my face,
Sentiment externalizing—
From inward apparition misting,
and cower me to a prostration—
But as crafty as the will of sin
keeps a hand in the pockets of my flesh—
He illustrates an active voice
in disagreement with you—
"WHY CAN'T I BE THE ONES WITH WINGS BEHIND YOU"
Striking
Azraels passionate nuclear ball of fire
on voice against you—
Instead
my panting shoulders hang weary
on the beaten track of free will—
Out flowing with thoughts
freely disappointing you
setting sail,
Please—
Efface me from the memory
of telepathic questioning,

In the present moment—
Eyes dried
knees dusted off
continuing Gods walk—
"MEN I HATE THOSE TEMPORARY DOUBTS IN DEEP THOUGHTS"

A Blink Of An Eye

In agreement with a blink of my eyes
you were conceived,
Times I've blinked with intoxicated happiness
swimming laps in my head,
and also times by means of physical suffering
stitching my soul constantly
without the anesthetic upon this testament—
In favor of poor sighted
flickering my eyes
to turn off radiant energy—
Anguishly blinking
the ages I had you in my presence
to know it's less then seven—
Your almost the age
of seven wonders in your world!
As I blink with jubilation,
Only in limitation
when ailment has no patience
sparing my black death thoughts—
I've been gone the entire heptad,
My heart in custody of distraught—
Secluded with
"If's" for reflections;
Like if only I had a second
to keep my eyes from blinking—
Absentee wouldn't be another sunny moment
dawning behind the horizon clouds,
Setting me away
from my sun Christian—
In A Blink Of An Eye.

If Only I Knew

If I could just sleep,
and rub my eyes when I wake—
Hello it's May,
I would understand why bears hibernate,
My dreams are worth more,
but deja vu is at best
I'll offer it for—
It's sad in the winters,
but I'll never understand
the enigma of polar bears
until I fly southward
along birds formation across winter tide,
The blows
of life's given birth
would need a turtle's shell
to show why I'm not slow—
But!!
Rabbits feet when I anticipate
the reasons why
my actions lands me in prison;
Perhaps my guess is–
This also explains
the selfish meticulous seconds
behind my sexual healing,
Before wings
I'll take hawks point of view—
Because
Long after wings are broken
philosophy continues to see
the point to that view—
Rich I'm not,
Unless richness of meaning–
Then I'm famous with the name
"DON AMOS"

Whichever leaves me far from nameless—
So depending on the sphere,
I'm a square that's a celebrity too—
If only I knew.

Earthquake In My Heart

As the floor shakes
the after shock accelerates
crashing waves against my heart—
I ponder
is another step safe
the more my chest expand
from the inhaling hymns
my sorrow heart sings—
My state of mind
continue my escape
while hearing it state;
"Why can't I stop"
As family dwelling aroma goes down
from crippling structure,
Panting breath—
Exhaling with begging air,
All the earmarks,
but I only ask
for eminence grace to protect their soul—
Past the invading storm
of screams and crys—
As if in Rwandas genocide days
under the heels of debris
from falling shacks,
At the same time—
"How Can I Stay"
Twisted in finger pinching pain
becoming my heartache
because I can't stay—
Envisioning the delicate butterfly aura,
My mother in that way—
At any rate
this foundation of my heart—
Won't cease from tremble flutter,

In and out of corners
avoiding features designed for loners
believing their goners
in possessed state of staring
stone house lowered as burial site
over warm blooded lineage and offspring,
Perhaps witchcraft or extreme inhabitant capacity
connected on Haiti's capital caused this—
Says the foam crevice lip of talkers,
Be that as it may—
Ginen the true knowledge
of Haitian culture,
and one sensitive essence
beyond words can question my attachment—
Mother's nature,
Finally standing still—
My stampede of million legged gazelles
escaping the hundreds
of legged prowler lioness'—
Releasing my lung imprisoned with air
after hearing the purity womb
that gave me entrance into a world—
Stood a test of time with existing breath,
but as the moon
allows the sun to rest—
Hope now worries my heart,
As I return to others—
Buried under shacks and debris.

A Boy Again

In either case the realm of reincarnation
blooms my spiritual essence
into a lotus flower—
A boy again would be the nature,
In front of TV's cartoon green grass
of bugs bunny's carrot eating life
the curious smiles of what comes next—
Rather than the rubbing
of two adolescent hands
behind mischievous grin
exploring and discovering mountains of VHS
that came with hidden ecstasies orgasmic treasures
on fathers porn collection,
But surely as the sun gives rise—
With certainty,
The days of crawling ground
would be developing strength
exerting the bicep for purpose
before a baby stands—
Preferred over the symptom of dry pupil
extra eyeing sexual actors misperceptions
of love's poetry
penetrating sexual actresses,
When instead
men caesura...
In the presence of blood moon cycles supposed curse
would I find comfort massaging
earth under mothers feet—
When stated with sick humor,
"I'm always under the ladies"
Than the belief
that unshaven pubic hair confirms I'm manly—
Forgetting the boy God made me,
Daddy look what I made of me—

Locked around men daily
running from what you stated,
"Now Can I Ask Your Thoughts Of Me"
Complete devotion
replace for painful awareness
of another's advantage,
Jealousy for envy—
Towards the siblings before me,
Feeling equal only—
When spankings the language,
In which place
bullies would have no language if for not
perceiving their affection
in the likes of home to me—
I'm scorn you see
or possibly just the boy in me
begging ears to hear
how childhood was confusing
towards inner maturity.

Butterfly That Got Away

The beat of wind dance butterflies away—
Contrasting my failed attempt
to catch the wing of one in a net—
Bringing winter rain glooms
caressing chill to sadden my skin—
Picturing color of love in your eyes
eloping my nerves
to dive into river of passion—
Where waterfall dripped
from the faucet of my armpits,
Skipping my heart to beats—
Bedazzled how beautiful
flower bloom standing still,
but balladhorn melody
press my eyes shut—
Trance in state of limbo
searching for notes my soul
ballets with piano console—
Whereby the cause
my awaken eyes imagining
a mythical dragon—
Exhaling flaming steam
press onto my ears before sudden awareness—
Another women's interest in Moi
sound like noise—
While in the midst of other neighborhood sounds—
I'm only wishing
this flying bee was me—
Securing the love for honey
to its Queen—
As cars whisk away day dreaming life
for frenzied out of tune saxophone,
and trumpet honking reality—
Despite nature's mercy

allowing me to sense you in a breeze—
Causing my eyes to swim fishes
down a lake over cheekbone valley,
Thoughts running marathon and triathlons—
And view of Blue Jay's
natural appearance soaring,
As key notes singing
"The Blues"
It's too late
when love sails
when a fools late,
but watching sunset boozing
until stars bring me your face—
Is real pain on a Tuesday,
Negating the light in my smile—
dimming to a frown,
Turning my heart brown
in harmony with waves
flying you away—
How can I explain
it's quiet where deers stay,
and a poisonous snake died
from pain through my vein it tasted,
It's growing colder each day
opening my eyes again,
but yet again—
The one that got away
put me here.

Angel Wings In Hell

The taste of blood is what you love,
So you starve yourself
howling in your days;
like related dogs—
Demanding me to follow
as contemptible you are—
Because I follow the spirit
dwelling in my heart—
I'm a ethereal in your world
that influence others in mines,
Not a reflection of you
exercising your power of vision
searching through my eyes—
Stoic to your words,
because of insight—
I stare longer at my faith
since it's the light promised
at the end of this road—
Demonic are your thoughts,
Combatting for my stay
in this dungeon place—
The closer the angels
wing me to my escape,
Your arms, I laugh—
Reaching what your hate seeks—
I'm free can't you see!
Confinement has nothing I wish,
Take away, What?
I have my mentality—
I can't feel well rested in here,
but of course
that's what you want for me,
Except—
God has a better plan

for the kids,
Clarifying—
There's not enough of me,
I can not choose you
over what I'm destined to be,
Hell is your misery—
Away I fly with angel wings.

Prisons Common—
$Wealth$

I'm sunken in a place
where my state is zombified physically,
Constant sound of a teaspoon
brush upon the lips of my ears—
Simply put,
I'm duplicated in images;
like the film
"GET OUT"
Produced by Jordan Peele—
But what's producing my comatose film
with image drooling
from the side of my lips—
Appears to be commonwealth as my enemy—
Convicting me to another realm of slavery,
Contrary to a thirteenth Amendment—
Thinking I'm hearing
violins constantly playing—
Doctor Martin's dreams,
Humming tunes of my ancestors melodies
for me to live free—
At the same time,
Chained in this open space yard
looking out pass the distance contemplating—
Am I also seeing what I'm hearing
a solo shadow playing a harmonica
I barely can see,
But clearly can hear—
This tombstone sentence is real,
Life History
doesn't disappear,
People like Bull Connor
deserved eternity in prison
for loving the intentions they did,

Witless was me!
In the mercy of many beats
playing the same tea spoon I missed—
Hypnotizing me,
Since adolescent
believing white skin
were actual Mastercard and Visa
in a world black skin
were products and commodities—
Urging!
Come purchase me;
like the painful knowledge
of Black History—
As if playing a game,
Waiting eagerly
trembling in bravado fear
with fingers submitting
on my second amendment—
Suicide
Unconsciously embedding anger
that exploded mistakenly from emotions
that made me feel Titanic's Iceberg—
Sinking me in a box
with many frozen water around me—
Hardly with time to breathe,
Now wanting to live
as the tears descend down
the shore of my jawline
in form of icicle illusion—
Ripping
through flesh I harden
with wrongful conviction—
Feeling how it hurts to bleed,
but this purpose I see
after celler mirrors revealed—
More youths

to drown from commonwealths
stroke of tea spoon—
Needing emancipations's
cardiopulmonary resuscitation (CPR)
before their bled by hypnosis racism—
Structurally on a prison plantation.

Black Male Butterfly

Upon my black wings—
Starting from my caterpillar years,
Cocooned comfortably
in my immigrant's womb—
No longer did I savor good quality
of natural Haitian nutrient culture,
Because energy I now felt
was constant prayer
keeping modern white K.K.K. shrouds away—
With their white sheet ideals,
Anger becoming her normal foriegn
emotional language I feel—
Can one imagine her crack cuticles
from chemicals
traveling like smoke
on evenings dinner bowl
through the nose,
Conceived with me,
but on the brink
giving me early birth,
because Marriott Enterprise—
Didn't believe in minorities
deserved maternity leave—
While theirs enjoyed cultivating
early stages of babies,
As I endured in toxic intoxication—
Kicking pain,
Coloring the grimace of sorrow
on her face,
because art of process food—
Takes time,
So she cried,
and I learned to breast stroke
in her somber tears—

Connecting her plight
with the thoughts of years
ancestors before her—
Here!
Picked cotton instead,
Rather bare knees laboring
over stained urine and defecation
for a philosophy that waged
an equal minimum—
Fraction design to subtract
fathers baritone happiness
in the comfort of belly vibration—
Poof! Like the smoke mirrors,
I appear understanding the years—
Why rubbing off the heartaches
under her feet gave me chills
of a Serbian wind,
but seeing the full circle—
"My Life Matter"
Imply to both skin
under red...white... and blue,
The balance of love—
Why the current of the wind blows
my red and blue colored wings
on the contradiction
of Thomas Jefferson's stone lips,
        "We hold these truths to be evidence
            that all men is created equal
            among these are Life, Liberty
            and the pursue of Happiness"
OR else give me death!
What else make sense—
Envisioning Old Testament
as Nat Turner did,
The exchange of peace—
Black Angel, Black Angel appeared

on his last breath given;
In the midst of my years—
America's finger as the system—
Noose around my neck,
While my spirit tip toe outwards
on faint breath,
Season that lingers the pollen
of injustice in the air—
My virtue dance in the wind
happily Black;
Like a butterfly.

My Skin Visits Me Black

These concrete lapses of time
has caused an eclipse
blocking the light to my reflections,
Until the conclusion of nano seconds
within mirror sight
became my dancing light behind a smile—
Realizing similar nose
when pyramids were yours—
Radiating in the flicker of sun's flame,
Knowing a lotus can rise
on prison grounds—
Exposing cracks confinement hides,
Crème de la Crème
when my inner nature accent
silver tongue Thomas Grays—
"Thoughts that breathe and words that burn"
For my wisdom structures
from an ancient pose
that links to sphinx,
and awareness how the sand storm feels
when spirits meet on the lines
of energy eloping through words
that kiss without the kiss—
There's bliss where tragedy exist
wrestling with hate to even see
what it loves—
Compliments to the mornings bosom sun
caressing the dark back
of night's sky
into orgasmic shooting stars—
Interpretation
in the presence of my skin
I cherish if ever theirs never a next,
Falling heir to the sense of indigenous—

Smoothing my ruffled brow
That once cared
in worlds trance for vanity—
In order to embrace
natural surroundings instead,
To a degree that daughters and sons—
Offspring of Eve
accepts the picture clear
as the nose on ones face
blown off Egyptian stone—
Crucifixion of a blackbird in a cage
owned by birds with whitethroat—
Ignoring the ignorance of gorillas
brought here like slaves,
Or Sean Carter expounding
what PROJECTS mean—
when Black Market is their trapping ways—
Epiphany by our ancestor
at four, four, four A.M.
Seeing that loving
every crack to my ass Black
cleansed me eternally—
Even in the event
pen cast me the enemy
many missed what God preserved in me—
Making my skin Black,
and pain the gain to escape,
When skin visits me Black, and explain.

Don Of Creation

Where my head rest—
On the open palms of Gods hand,
Certitude support the visions—
I envision with a thousand butterflies
folk dancing
on the wings of your smile;
like my heart tap dancing—
Watching the contemporary art
of birds happy dashing
their walk on air,
I am bless—
With view beyond each horizon's
source of light,
Where canaries are singing
a fathers love song
for Elijah Don.

Midnight Plight

What of my plight—
Seen as not structurally racist,
In contemplation of my struggle soaring
on land that's free;
Like the beautiful fragile wings
of a painted lady—
Soaring across an oppressive wind,
Yet,
What is seen, an angry Black man.

Beyond The Coast Of My Wrongful Conviction

My simple ethnic marker—
Now subject as a felon,
Denoting my status;
like days of negro,
As each day grows,
Furthers—
Distance from my wrongful conviction,
Lies the shore along my eyes drying;
like a thirsty desert
burning under the sun—
Is it because I'm stout;
like a maroon,
I labor
hard in erect industrial building,
and the essence of colonial legislatures—
Linger: on the breath,
Inherited by systemic racism descendants—
Perhaps,
for showing silence only my heart see—
When Black drug dealing conquistadors—
Aimed,
I was a victim too!
And because of my hue
against the lost of their hue—
Deemed me fit
for their generational plantation–
Established many crescent moons ago,
When wondering thoughts;
like myself today,
Sailing on this ocean
with middle passage mind—
Commonwealth recognizing:
The legality of slavery—
Perpetual and heritable—

Their privilege right—
Stringing my six amendment
on trees harmless error—
Despite fruit from a poisonous tree,
My guilt—
Lie on the root
of perpetual slavery,
Beyond the coast
of my wrongful conviction.

Black Fabric

Skin soil;
like the fine earth—
Where I dug deep
beyond my outer layer,
Into a world—
Mostly streaming of
aquatic celestial—
I discovered the hands
of my ancestors labor,
The seeds planted,
and blossoming;
like agricultural freedom—
The sewing of a Black culture—
"L' Union Fait La Force"

Behind Black Eyelids: prt.1

We sleep to only stay awake—
By the alarming nightmares of—
Handsome son he is
dark chocolate;
Like mocha—
Barely old enough
to trick or treat alone
at the door of puberty,
But there—
The reality of an old face storm—
Preserved,
Waiting thirstily
with fang drawn—
Whisking black lives away;
like Emmit Til,
and our ancestors
"GONE WITH THE WIND"
Another black hue—
Mobbed by the hands
of quote on quote—
"He Whistled"
and then
"He Reached"
Black mothers awaken by horror—
Shaken,
Embraced by realities tears.

Behind Black Eyelids: prt.2

In the comfort of our sleep—
We assemble,
In a place Mass Incarceration
symbolize Jim Crow days,
Where hope—
Dilly dally under wax moonlight—
Echoing our thoughts in unity,
Needing freedom to be us,
Idiom language
for the color of our skin,
Seeking—
Disarming youths
with dream speeches—
Our communities trusting black harmony,
Smiling the mile;
like a garden of daisies—
Reflecting in the change we've become...
MATTERS!

The Falling Leaf Speaks

Stolen seeds replanted,
Carry on in a land
as we blossom—
Back snapping;
like branches,
Drowning in the cries
of our protest,
We ask—???
Let our years
be the pure water drunk
from your privilege dinner cups—
Hear our bitter taste of salt,
and kneel
on seeds peppered on the ground—
Crawl with the pain of reflection,
but off our necks—
And hear the silence speak...
No Justice No Peace!

Black Candle Wax

Flame above my head—
Flickers my pain,
Devilish fire
leaving black forest in ashes—
Face against concrete;
Oppression by knee—
"I can't BREATHE"
Conjuring voice
Eric Garnered,
My wax tears dripping—
Another,
As we sing candles in hand—
We Shall Over Come.

River Across High Cheek Bones

This river runs red,
Shackling ebony skin ankles—
Onto grief,
Snuffing the wind—
From Black handsome communities,
Losing birth to the hands
written by White reapers venom words—
STAND YOUR GROUND!
Yet
From river lava running red—
Maya Angelou's poetic words—
"Still We Rise"
Liquid and dust—
Into Bkack Lives—
Matter, The reason WE CRY.

Faith

Faith do you wander
past the distance
as my mind,
Is it—
I gave up on you,
and I now live outside your fingers—
Pointing my directions,
Moving streams of obstacles
seeking to bound me in lust—
Where my many laps confine
are walks talking about everything,
but nothing at all—
Your scorn making my sitting area
on a butt pinching bucket,
Awareness,
Releasing my souls emotions poetically—
Where your love
awaits me with open limbs,
Conquering the storm of my fears
with liberty's rays—
Comforting my walk in your counsel,
For your judgment is only the matter—
I fell in love with FAITH.

One American Hue

The rage of fire within me—
Has been snuffed out
with the water of love,
I can't change the hills
of my ancestors—
Also the decor I'm skinned in,
Sweet berry
behind reflection—
My colored hand looking to reach
into the hearts of hate,
and plant new seed of Love—
OR continue watering
the green grass of Peace,
Martin pastured through Christ—
The equality of squeezing a fruit
from the same tree,
and receiving the same juice—
And even though
the culture of apples
are not pears—
As humans
we understand the soil
of their roots remain the same—
Am I not human enough for redemption,
From my own ignorant oppression?
Shall my childish way
forever silence my maturity through Hope?
Am I forsaken to inspire humanity
to see one another
through the lens of Love?
Even Faith can see
the river of freedom—
Streaming down on the face
of Mt. Rushmore when it rains,

The rainbow above Martin's statue
long after the closing clouds fade—
And brings one progressive America,
Wading in the water.

The Sound Of Hove When Freedom Calls

I no longer sleep,
and for this—
My spiritual journeys are protected
on the dust of egg shells—
Guiding me,
Sojourner seeking freedom,
also for the spirits of white allies—
Once against pro slavery;
like Anthony Benezet—
Where can I still find
these morale compass,
Have they gone to sleep—
Knowing this liberty bell
yearns to be rung,
Again—
Loud enough for their conscious
to rise its breast like a peacock,
In the face of contradiction
if all human are me in essence,
Yet!
Unlawfully my conviction
is placed in a slave coffle,
Leaving behind a lake—
Birth by my tears petition,
What am I,
If not Except—
For a crime as punishment?
Which ancestors plight
have I inherited—
Whereof
this party shall have been
Wrongfully duly convicted?
For days and nights awoke,
and awaiting—

The sweet melody
of Mintys transition
into Harriet Tubman—
Now The Conviction Intergrity Program—
Sitting still on water...
Until the sound of my hove
come galloping;
like my ancestors to freedom.

Black Flesh, Pure Heart

The calm—
Before storm possessed my flesh,
By the river
I fell—
In the hands of baptism,
A believer bequests
in the great commission—
Poetically,
Releasing my nubian woman
from ways—
Seven demons possessed
Mary Magdalene.

Tree Of Structural Racism

My first breath
accepted Americas hand,
but on this same tree—
Communities branched out
in handsome Black faces—
The features of elders
wore wrinkles of sorrow,
and gray clouds of wisdom
hovered over their Black experience,
and depending on the autumn season—
A few black leafs
would linger to listen—
While the winter of structural racism
colonized the black leafs
that fell into slavery—
Listen!
the elders vociferously whispered—
About an America
home of brave natives—
Who withered away
by drunkard confusion;
like black communities today
gated with liquor fences—
Toes-Tipping past moonlight
branch to branch
in search for manufactured poppy seeds—
Schools speaking nothing of Juneteenth,
OH SAY CAN YOU SEE!
BY the dawn's setting light—
Our Black
Red and Green flag
was there—
Our uncles,
brothers and fathers

from branch to branch—
Were welcomed by lynch mobs
with grim smiles,
It is there—
I see the redlining
around every tree,
Mass Incarcerated for segregation,
Backward education
attacking our nation—
It is also there
sun rises
with spirit elders whispered,
Far when I wouldn't listen—
BLACK LIVES MATTER!
Branch together,
and uproot—
The Tree Of Structural Racism.

Boston Brown Bread

My concrete walks
were hard on contradiction—
Even on the nature
of Black and White—
Amid the racist voices
so quick to spread oppressive lies—
You should have seen
those lily-white flowers bloom
on a Dead End Street
named Hesston Terrace,
And White neighbors
did not act like strangers—
Yet,
I am painfully aware
of the years before my birth
to the eighties—
Ten years to be exact,
A time of visionary dreams
court ordered bussing
by using the pen to paint
a pretty picture
in the face of an ugly truth,
Integrating South Boston public school—
Revealing racial tension lain dormant
beneath the skin,
but where I lived
was named Dorchester—
And Amillia
an old white lady
older than the seventies—
Her walk so angelic
when she often offered duplex cookies—
To fit strings in between needle holes,
Pulling me into a world like the thread

I would pass
through the eye of a needle—
The opposite end of a truth
that stings;
Like seeing through the eyes
of Boston's first Blacks,
How they arrived in noose like chains—
Forced tightly around their necks,
Every one of them
bruised, battered and bound
below the bloodstained decks of Desirè's
first American built slave ship—
Ironically enough,
A name spelled
with French accent—
Maybe to disguise
or not
this prominent port—
The shores of Boston
used like bait
for human slaves—
As their eyes glazed open;
like fish being swapped—
Horror to repeat
bitter before sweet—
So am I wrong to believe
that Barbara
a white hippy or same gender kisser
with bouncing golden retriever hair—
Reflected
the hearts and minds
of Boston's board selectman—
Waging political war to end slavery,
As if not history?
The very days I played so freely
on Barbara's lush green property;

like mid eighteenth century Blacks—
Becoming ten percent of Boston's populace,
and moving as a free community
formed in the growing neighborhood
of New Guinea—
Now known as North End,
But then—
When did one end?
And the other begin?
Knowing Guinea
is a West African land
colonized by France—
Desirè
unloaded her human cargo,
Today—
Where mostly Italians live,
Where New Guinea
would sound derogatory to them—
Change made sense,
But,
Unlike Blacks
inheriting the N-word—
I was first labeled
by a Black skin—
Redesigning a social disgrace
to justify this,
Oxymoron not to see—
Fortunately
history for me did not repeat—
White church goers on Pleasant Street
nearly begged us as kids
come and see
what Black Jesus did for me—
Only to experience media coverage,
Inflaming me to feel
what I rather not believe—

Ninety-nine percent
what Whites think
is equivalent
to the one percent's racist laden fear,
Truthfully—
My parents never mentioned this—
I often heard them say
to beware,
because they feared—
Our Black and Hispanic neighbors,
Who were like the kids
in my grade school—
Bullying me for being Haitian,
and a bit too nice to say—
FUCK YOU!
Clearly—
The forty-four Blacks
founding the African Society—
Boston's only Black owned property,
Where rhythm and blues swung hips to move—
Was not the world I knew,
Whites were the nice kids—
Ronny and Danny,
and Scotty's mother
was nice too—
Even as elementary's lunch mother,
And yes—
It makes me sad
to know about Frederick Douglas—
The way he faced public insults,
Forced to sit
in Jim Crow sections on trains—
That steamed across his eye brows
when boarding in Lynn,
A rail of history to come—
Following

to the end dooms to repeat it—
Maybe not physically,
but second thoughts
thinking out loud
make it hard
not to act foolishly;
Like Boston gangs—
Committed to kill one another
for history they never lived,
Though—
Never part of their childhood,
I can still understand how they feel—
How should one honestly think,
If one is constantly linked
to Black lynching,
And those beatings on TV—
Should they not be trusted
as a measure of reality?
But what of my history?
Is it not important for peace—
A white custodian
who allowed me to eat
graham crackers and milk—
Long after school was dismissed,
According to Charles Sumner's argument—
A rite of passage closely related,
Parallel
to the successful Thurgood Marshall's—
Brown-versus-Board of education,
Dated more than a hundred years prior,
Which led me to earn—
My Cahill award,
Learning what miss Cahill had taught—
Adding and subtracting
not only in math,
But may I ADD—

Late eighteen hundred,
Boston had a Black city council;
like today's Haitian Ruthzee—
Commercialize these images always, please
on television—
As if knowing
Eureka Cooperative Bank
was less than—
Knowing whites lived in Savin Hill,
Racial discrimination exists
when the shoe doesn't fit,
But if Blacks can not find peace
amongst their own skin—
Under the weight of a neighborhood label,
South End House and Robert Gould Shaw housings—
Is it wrong for whites
to think Blacks
run from their own skin?
Well,
My Boston life
encountered more progressive Whites—
And in case I failed to mention,
I always felt welcomed
in Savin Hill—
Especially the seasons
when I randomly shoveled
for twenty dollar bills—
There's no doubt
how easily I could've been supported
by Whites;
Like Black politician Mel King—
Who ran for Mayor
nineteen seventy-nine—
Is no wonder
why Michelle Wu—
My Mayor today,

makes me a proud
Boston Brown Bread.

A Sista's Attitude

The world doesn't owe me nothing,
but your kind sure do hate to offer,
Maybe because it's mines from starter—
So if I snap my finger and role my neck
it's not because I'm Black—
It's because a Sista has the right
to talk about that—
so pay me the acre and mule
if I'm going to work that hard
around men that hawk with brains that rot,
I'm born to be a partner
my ideas come from the same father—
Yet you act like a bastard
when I'm climbing the chains
right beside you—
So like the wiser
I step back in order to strut
right pass where your brain is at—
Yes, the effect caused the idea MAN-I-Can,
but all you see is a mannequin,
My ideas come from suffering—
Inspiration from you judging Blacks,
and the Sistas
are only good for touching
from the moment I did nothing—
Bet you never seen this lawsuit coming—
"That Bitch!"
No, that's the Sista in me—
The one a brotha may miss because
I'm darker than his TV or what's on TV.
I lick my lips from terse
to value what my ears thirst,
My hips swaying to the beat
of Oxford dictionary words,

Intoxicated by how it works—
So I'll always have a response
to your every words,
Hello Sista,
I'm know better than a prostitute
when I sleep with men
without marriage or commitment,
Hello Sista,
I'm know better than a stripper
when my dress is a cleavage away
from exposing treasure—
Take my hand,
and let's weather this storm together,
I know a place
the sun shines a lot more better—
Mountains dry enough to climb more further,
Nature speaks the language
your spirit answers—
Confidence a weak man can't shelter—
So a walk in the rain
makes me feel a lot more better—
You see where I'm heading?
Ignore the hooting and hollering
of john's and pimp daddies
around this corner—
See that Sista,
Sista and Sista
that see us striving down this boulevard—
Make a purpose to head back
to the weathered storm,
Hello Sista,
You to Sista,
and bring that Sista—
I know a place
that men say hello
with roses to a Sista,

Dignity exposed to a Sista,
Equality see no color in a Sista—
Make no mistake
we're all Sistas
lost in our own mistakes,
but over this mountain—
There's no mistake God creates,
Sahara, mother Africa—
Even she
has a Sistas attitude like no other,
See Kwanzaa celebrates our culture—
Hello C. Delores Tucker,
Maya Angelou,
Oprah Winfrey,
and so many others
depending who you wonder,
No blue singing in this here avenue—
Strictly equal revenue—
Hear the drums they beat for you
tribal clothes
the color of rainbows to represent you—
Sista, welcome to a new you—
Go ahead strut
whip your hair loose
see your virtue—
Black enterprise respects you,
Ebony born—
Jet sees your skin and beauty within,
Enough dignity to win magazine publishing—
A Sista might be the next Black president—
There's enough Black networks
                              to follow
                                    the trend—

You remember that Sista that spread wisdom
through King Kong literature,
What a poetic gesture

a breath of substance—
You think the brothas get her?
A perfect reason to stay away
from ANN Coulter's—
We Sistas see racist in all sections
Republicans
Democrats
even Liberal standards—
We started Black Panthers
and every section white racist
politicked was Black gangsta's—
Sista,
she think we're strangers,
America doesn't have more Black criminals
than our government!
All Blacks aren't innocent,
but we do share one interest—
I know that's right Sista—
There's a disproportionate number of
young white criminals too—
Let's not act like fools—
Sista,
she's already old news—
We need to figure out how to keep more
young Sista's in school—
The Sistas in Hidden Figures
might have a clue—
Sista,
now you're acting like a fool—
Sista,
Laughing keeps my skin from crackin'
how Jesus did facing disaster,
and also scripted
wise can play the fool,
but fool can no way play wise—
Our young Sista's need spiritual guide,

A place in every State
Sista's unite,
and prosperous Sista's come by
to help bring their spirits to life—
Or young rappers and street brothas
will verbally attract Sistas that feel forgotten
with lifestyles that seem attractive
cause poor tastes nasty—
A place Sistas can ask a brotha
if it was their sister—
A place Sistas can express
that young Sista's ideas make sense,
Their own riches are better than leeching—
Eye candy for the moment isn't,
Rappers are really dissing
like Liberals act they wasn't lynching
back in the fifties—
                    LISTEN!
Toussaint L'Ouverture is the party we're missing—
Black votes are mistreated
for lack of history
about who freed us in the Western Hemisphere—
Face it,
Racist existed,
but not more than Democrat Dixies—
Sista's,
crack a book
you'll see what TV'S switching—
There's enough Sista's
to get this subject kicking,
A wise brother once said
"I HAVE A DREAM THAT ONE DAY,"
but who voted against that???
Sista,
your sweating your perm out,
but I understand—

Segregationist was DEM-CATS—
Sista,
That's where I rest my case at—
Let's talk about sex life,
Well,
I need a man right?
Where's Amos head at?
Sista,
we're talking about ACE right?
The past doesn't represent new light—
Plus he expressed that
Jesus saved his wretched life,
Action is his best fight
against action that mirrored his past life—
So Sista,
If God is with that
who can be against that?
Jesus understand he's Black—
Where you think some of his early years
were spent at?
Africa where Moses was birth at—
Even Joseph chose to rest at,
and Saxons failed to mention that
the whole civilization was Black—
Sista,
Black history goes back—
How about once leading people on Earth,
Egypt all Black
name derived from Blacks, Ethiopia,
of all that—
pioneers,
science,
architecture,
medicine,
writing,
first to build in stone, et cetera—

Don't ask what happened,
Our focus is to unite us—
So Africa can once again be ours,
and drop slave names for ours;
like Queen Nefertari and Hatshepsut the Great—
Even they had a Sista's way—
Sista,
I can't see them this way!
Well Sista,
that's what history tried to erase,
but feminine charms
originates from your race—
One of the reasons
other nations wanted a taste and raped—
Imagine your curves on them in those days,
Make no mistake
how they lust in modern days—
Sista,
if that's the case
why do brotha's crave other race?
Sista,
Let's bring the young Sista's to seek
Amos to educate.
ACE,
that's your name?
Sista,
I understand what they say,
but Amos is my real name—
So what's your case,
Black men lustig women from other race—
Sista,
Rain flooded our ways
long before today—
Love only exists in minds today,
All women are Sista's through love
if I say—

Time should teach brotha's to stay
with one
rather than repeating what is done—
Sista,
we dream too much,
and miss what's in front—
Love is what makes us one,
Not what the one percent wants us to discuss—
Let's take a walk,
See that brotha selling drugs
he's missing love—
A color conversation
would help him miss it more—
Don't mind the gun toting thugs,
They have love,
but lack to share with us all—
Being Black is their excuse
for being thugs—
Sista,
some Blacks are lost,
and race is not the cause—
I'm them that chose to reach to God,
so I lust because I love—
Take my hand so I can show
what butterflies and birds have on us,
A beautiful world they accept as a gift
bird song is how they cheer—
Doves don't kill doves,
and hate blue jays for looking great
we're all humans in this place,
Love should only be the case—
Sista,
You still think he's Ace?
Sista,
he's great,
but love will have to wait

he's engaged in the same work
we're into these days—
Like helping Sista's heal
the way his helping brotha's
redeem back into their place—
There's many Sistas blind
from broken heart lies—
That's where my love resides
helping Sista's decide
poor is not right—
Vulnerability only excites
blood thirsty enemies
like politicians split
from keeping us from equality—
Sista,
Where are the initiatives for speaking logically
if actions cease to exist?
My heart beats with every speech—
Sweat bleeds out my skin when heat rises
deep down from ancestor's genes—
Sista,
We're made to unite—
Can't you see
that's the initiative
they want us to miss,
A march to feed babies overseas because
"Black Lives Do Matter,"
not just here—
Sista,
too many whites run the development agencies
allowing communities to be bluntly racist
with oxymoron statements—
Denying integration on free land
they claim
our young Sista's unfit in their class
on live NPR'S

"Frontline"
Even their children are brainwashed
to be racist in McKinney, Texas—
Oh goodness gracious!
Sista,
This journey will shed many tears
before true happiness is granted—
But let's make this happen
for young Sista's facing disasters
that find courage to share what happened,
When a young Sista's goal—
Is to become a Black women's dreams
prosperous living
a big house with picket fence,
and all the trimmings—
A vision overcoming the odds,
and always aim for the stars,
Queen to his King,
but never realizes
how much pain love can bring—
"That first kiss!"
Ooh, that first kiss,
Full of passion and bliss—
You couldn't tell her nothing,
because she thought she knew love
was suppose to feel like this—
Shy at thirteen,
but with him
she was certain—
Til he got what he wanted
"she's no longer a virgin"
Used and abused,
and tossed to the side—
Doing whatever he said
on the nights that she cried—
To her parents

she lied,
and from friends
she'd hide—
Giving all her love to him,
and now broken inside,
Her period is late—
Who can she face
when he says it's not his,
and put her through hell—
And word around is
she's a slutty girl,
and her thoughts have no one to trust
naive being the cause—
So excuse her
for snapping her neck,
because most men are dogs,
and deserve no respect—
All the pain that she felt!
Where was he
when she was crying for help?
Stuck with his kids,
and no food on the shelf—
Running the streets and leaving her for self,
because you talk sweet,
and expect her to listen—
Well,
She played the fool for too long,
A good girl while his ass was gone—
Forced to drop out of school
now dealing with welfare,
Until she found who else cared—
Sista's like Lashawn who found
"Success Her Way,"
and made it her well fare—
Who else cares,
Shouldn't be the only answer

when you can be the next her—
Gathering Sista's
to free Sista's from mental slavery—
From men who don't care—
Leading Sista's away
from Tina Turner's nightmares,
and embrace their Sista's attitude crisis—
To end this terrible crisis.

Co-written with Steven Webster

My Son's Shoes

With tears I wish my dad
was a bit more here,
but then again—
I'm just a kid
turning into a teen—
Realizing
my step daddy
is not even my kin,
and now left seeking to connect—
With just flick through pictures,
I wonder...
If he even remembers
we laid in peace—
What kind of man leaves his kid—
When only I have visions
of wishing I'm swinging from his reaches
which brings me inches—
Closer to the sound
of his heart beating
from how he embraces me,
but then I'm saddened
from the thoughts
that make it feel like a secret—
Because nobody shares
Who He Is or Where He Is,
and I'm too shy
to show interest why I smile—
When they link my resemblance to his—
OR link a random gift
Angel Tree said he sent,
Appearing once a year;
like the mysterious Saint Nick—
When Kwanzaa is the Kuu-mba
that I yearn,

because I want to learn—
If it's because of him
basketball is where I turned,
or my immature behavior—
I tend to hear
mother say from him—
When Google say he killed!
Do you understand how I feel—
His not here to explain
those moments I hate
what I hear—
Making me feel
my step daddy
is more authentic than him,
because prison blocks his true identity—
And I'm left to wonder,
If "LIFE"
the same life
he blessed me with,
but decided not to take me...
OR will I inherit—
That "LIFE"
from my surname
attached to this shoe
I leave unlace...

Eleven Years Of Lashes

Clearly!
I'm a free man
the naked eye can't see—
Endured slave tactics,
That connects me to the whips
that lifted skins of Black men,
When I was ten—

Lashes! Lashes!
You f@#king bastard,
but not exactly in english—
But I get it,
My behaviors
rebelling against masters,
and my only hope is
he never lynch's me,
because
I've become accustom
to whips that leaves
tire marks on skin
with speed bumps
the length of snake skin
that amaze me—
For I no longer flinch
when it hits—
Cause I'm in tune
with the sound it zippppppppps
through the wind,
And suddenly I feel heat
starting from my feet—
Risingggggggg through my body
making my head itch,
Because
I knew belts better than fashion—

The buckles on them
were more drastic,
and Sundays were for laughing (ha,ha,)
because
master could not find ones
that blasted,
cause
I would hide them—
Causing my knees
to hit grainers for hours
made for shredding natural condiments
that tore through my flesh—
Holding over my head—
A Rock
heavy enough to crack my neck,
But still
I was a bad slave—
In and out of markets
that stored video game cartridge
I stole for me and my brothers—
Until white Supremacy cuffs me,
and release me to a master
that bites when he beats me—
While trying to see
if I'll withstand the blow from a TV,
By then—
What the hell could child strength
cause to my skin—
First sign of trauma
was on cats instead—
And
I'm impress my ears,
Still hears—
From years
it's been twist
into pain cauliflower gives—

The faucet in my eyes
has... finally... run... dry—
For I am angered
that I'm whipped
to walk straight
in the likes of baby calfs
in foreign States—

WHO CAN EXPLAIN MASTERS WAY!

When knuckles come across my face
for being out late,
and my brain
is being knocked each and every way
at that age—
See
I only prayed in church
not to get the pinchhhhhhhh
that can compete with
Holy Ghost Spirit
for thinking I can speak—
While pastors preaching
the Christian Religion—
Tactic that also kept my lips seal...
When "D.C.F."
Slave ship came fishing—
Because kidnapping
was their mission
to give masters
worst than I witnessed—

But Lashes! Lashes!
Did not
typically make me a bastard,
Because—
I knew

my master was also a father—
Uneducated,
Sharing what his master
imposed on him—
That white supremacist masters
oppressed on them—

Plus, huh...
I never bent—
Rather
at sixteen
I flexed on him—
And experience
became computer chips
linking to the origin of me—
DNA
white Supremacy seek to understand—
Why Haitian blood is so fierce—
Despite those years of Lashes—
Still not broken within,
but evolved into a right man
without razor Mark's to my skin—
OR rather lashing back
with machine gun—
Clipping away nice kids in classes,
and say
because I heard voices—
Listen to my voice please,
I forgive those lashes
that derived from
white Supremacy skin—
Knowing liberation
is the true meaning
why I'm Haitian.

Morning Why

I can ask why,
but will that answer
the ends to my cries,
Morning sun of sorrow—
Walking through my door
without halo,
Troubling my smile—
As it lingers,
Agony of a thousand dirty needles
puncturing my skin,
and my thoughts
finding the tears
burning away snow
resting under my feet
as it drips—
Looking at your still image,
I'm frozen—
With gruesome weather
if ever I'll unfreeze,
and my soul allowed to grief properly—
At this cliff I sit—
I've been pushed physically,
but my spirit sit—
Watching the repeating grins
off my misery
pass by like clouds
in turn pushing me—
Where I only wish
I never caused anyone strife—
So this affliction
wouldn't make it their day,
My mother—
Beautiful as this morning day,
Forever gone they say—

Will I crawl in this wilderness eternally—
Hearing hyenas laugh as night creep
away with her last morning smile—
But here you are,
365 moons later—
I hear no wolves
howling the grief I seek,
and there goes a glimpse
of blue sky, I think—
You smile instead,
Awed—
By sun shinning again
without morning whys instead.

What I Think

What I think
knowing family cares
to see me do well—
One wouldn't wish me hell,
but I would still cry
as if I'm marked for hell,
Yes! I do cry,
because I remember
mothers tears
when her father moved on—
So it slays me
to even think—
Tears she'll shed if my death
neared right before her eyes,
Unbeknownst as a child—
Mothers favorite saying
"God if this child is cursed kill it in my womb,"
Kept me a believer
being birth to hear this—
Who would ever believe this,
Dark nights would convert my face
into skull sights,
Soft skin easily penetrated
by bullies and lose God's sight,
Oh!
Now out of my right mind;
like Adam and Eve—
Recognizing
payless are bo-bo's to me,
Brand name clothes
aren't purchased at K-Mart
or Targets you see,
The reason why I walk
pigeon toe like this—

Mother had an accident
when I was in her womb you see—
Fib mother told me,
I always believed—
Which made them laugh and
point more at my stupidity—
So I stole
my parents hard earn money you see,
To change my appearance you see,
but I continued to smell
foriegn you see—
Haitian ancestry
picking more fights for me—
Ending on the boulevard
of small classes
segregated kids considered S.P.E.D. classes,
Funny thing—
I was now divided
into a group of mirrors
reflecting my pain
no matter how it came—
Without names
you know how my life became—
Running with the insane,
Drugs, Guns
pierced ears with braids
tattoos with weird phrase—
Everything my parents' disgrace,
but still I prayed,
because Saturdays at church felt good,
Gospel concerts with Unity Mass Choir
gave me a high marijuana couldn't,
but the devil was never to far behind—
With just a whisper
misdirected back into foolishness,
Far from a poison heart through faith,

but pain became torture—
Not wanting to experience
pass childhood ways from others—
Still thanks to my mother
I was able to treat girls;
like my sisters and goddaughters,
Thanks to my mother
I know how to love,
Thanks to my mother
I know God
is my one true love,
Thanks to my mother
however I faltered,
She still loves—
Mobilizing good she instilled in me,
Buried so deep over soft skin,
Only the belief in trifecta—
Could guide me back
to my youthful spirit,
Yes! that's what I think
I owe my family.

Water From My Rose

She found me under a rock—
Where I was succumbed to be,
and even though the air
was different from
the for granted one I took—
I found comfort in piling up
a mound of dirt
to pillow my head,
Where ants paraded
with instruments in hand
for a castle was built
as my body lay still,
and when I thought
about my transgression—
My cries cascaded
into a river—
Giving way as both
worms and slugs
bathe in tempo; like baptism way,
and it was behind echoes
of why I cried—
The constant knock
louder than her trumpet woes
yielding her hearts river flow
to suddenly cease,
and see
where our two streams revealed—
Lifting this rock
previously where her faced laid,
and we both reached
to wipe dust burden over our cheeks,
I became still—
Tasting my tears
being her sweetest water

speaking to me.

Free Me From Reality

The weight of my mind
carried my soul
through non-existing mud—
Seeking the difference
between Holy ghost and Spiritual love—
Chasing me
to hear the chains without the cuffs,
Is there a meaning
my heart ticks like a clock,
but I waste it on realities thoughts—
Missing why nature is connected to us,
and the wind
the reflection of us
when God speaks to us,
Is death not a forgiveness
when a second notice on earth
can become hell—
A woman suffers
giving birth can't you tell—
Perhaps death is just a feeling
the world imprison us to feel I feel,
but the pain in reality is real—
Sickness becomes disease,
but there's a place
mind believe tranquility exist—
From distraction that kills
the spirit in me—
Time after time
I conjure heaven to me—
Meditation is the key
making death easier
to live in eternity,
but my dreams keeps me prisoner
in this reality when I sleep—

In order to awaken
and chase fantasy—
Having nothing to do
with the journey enlightening me—
Into a bulb as bright
as the stars galaxy,
When nights become vision
my mind see—
Connecting money, seductive fornication
to the reason I sin
just to fit in this essence that kills—
When only I want to be free of,
Emotions and concepts—
Imprisoning me into a space
of natural simplicity,
Missing the essential
to bliss and clarity—
Free me from reality.

About The Author

Born and raised in Boston, Massachusetts to Haitian parents, where it was hard embracing my ethnic culture, because I wanted to fit in with black and brown Americans in my community. The difference in culture, despite me sharing the same hue as them, led to bullying and ultimately unfocus in school. At the early ages in elementary's 3rd grade I noticed I loved reading and writing. I started developing ideas for storytelling. Unfortunately, my insecurity and distraction from school led me to fitting in with the neighborhood bullies until anger took a hold of me and eventually contributed to my incarceration.

After losing my freedom, I began to pursue my education on my own. Reading became key to unlocking me from ignorance. Later I enrolled in the prison education programs and successfully earned certificates from Spectrum's (Criminal Thinking) and the NEADS Dog program.

Nowadays I enjoy educating myself on my Haitian culture, writing short (fictional) stories, and performing the art of Spoken Words Poetry, which I would love to share with you all. Enjoy reading!

Sincerely,
Amos Don